Dear Sir / Madam,

on the following pages you will find a
variety of colored, vintage advertisement
ephemera pieces.
You may be wondering what you can do
with them? Here are a few ideas:
Use them in your journals, planner and
altered art projects. Decorate cards, design
scrapbook layouts and make your own em-
bellishments. The possibilities are endless...
Remember that you are an artist. You
can NOT mess up your projects, only make
them more beautiful by making them yours.
Use the images to fuel your creativity
and use them as inspiration.
Thank you for buying this book and I hope
you have a fantastic time using it.
Happy Crafting

Dorothe
designer and fellow crafter

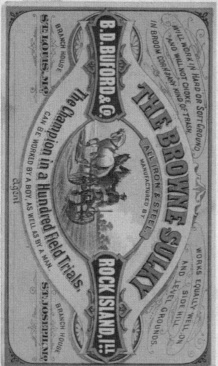

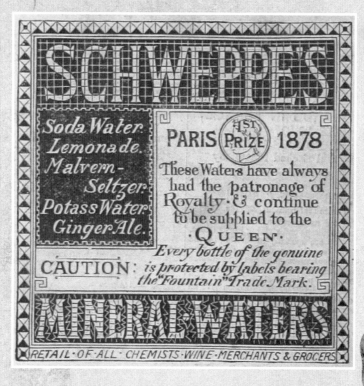

Cacao
en
Chocolaad
A:Driessen

PARFUM
LARIETTE
L.T. PIVER
PARIS

BACK ACHE QUICKLY RELIEVED
BY CARTER'S
Smart Weed & Belladonna
BACK ACHE PLASTERS

SEE OTHER SIDE

NATURE'S LAXATIVE PLEASANT
SYRUP FIGS
MANUFACTURED BY CALIFORNIA FIG SYRUP Co.
SAN-FRANCISCO, CAL.
LOUISVILLE, KY. NEW YORK, N.Y.

Drexel's
BELL COLOGNE

C. Meyer & Co
Sole Proprietors,
BALTIMORE, MD.
U.S.A.

Hall's VEGETABLE SICILIAN HAIR RENEWER

Saved Father's Hair from turning gray,
and falling off, and will save yours
and keeps the scalp healthy.
THE PEOPLES FAVORITE

SYRUP OF FIGS

PETER'S THE ORIGINAL Milk Chocolate

Delicious, yet wholesome;
Rich, yet digestible.

SOAP
B.T. BABBITT'S BEST SOAP
PET OF THE HOUSEHOLD.

CACAO KARSTEL

LONGINES
el mejor reloj
de precisión
De venta en todas las
buenas relojerías.

Increase trade at your fountain by dispensing the
delicious, refreshing beverage,

Coca-Cola

No fountain bever-
age ever increased
in popularity so
rapidly.
None will draw so
many customers to
your fountain.

Advertising matter from any branch free.
THE COCA-COLA CO.,
Atlanta.   Chicago.   Dallas.   Philadelphia.   Los Angeles.

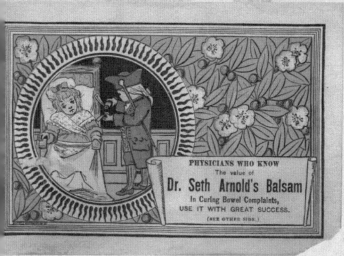

PHYSICIANS WHO KNOW
The value of
Dr. Seth Arnold's Balsam
In Curing Bowel Complaints,
USE IT WITH GREAT SUCCESS.

(SEE OTHER SIDE.)

LADIES' PERFUMED CALENDAR

1895

COMPLIMENTS OF
E.W. HOYT & CO.
LOWELL, MASS

PROPRIETORS OF
HOYT'S GERMAN COLOGNE   RUBIFOAM FOR THE TEETH.

CHOCOLATES
Y DULCES
MATÍAS LÓPEZ

LOS QUE TOMAN DOS VECES
AL DÍA EL CHOCOLATE DE LÓPEZ.

DESPUÉS DE TOMAR EL CHOCOLATE
DE LÓPEZ.

ANTES DE TOMAR EL
CHOCOLATE DE LÓPEZ.

MADRID-ESCORIAL. Oficinas, Palma alta, 8 MADRID.

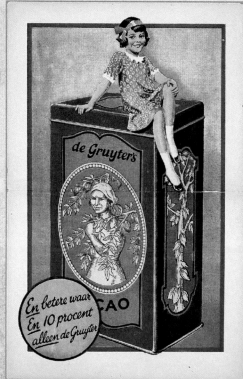

de Gruyter's

CAO

En betere waar
En 10 procent
alleen de Gruyter

Radam's Microbe Killer
Malt Extract

Long Island Bottling Co.
BROOKLYN, N.Y.

CORRIERE DELLE
SIGNORE

8 pagine in 4
settimanali

ricche d'incisioni
ed
elegante modello
tagliato

FIGURINO
COLORATO
in prima pagina

e 8 pagine
staccate
d'uno dei romanzi
più interessanti
del giorno
ANNO L 5
C 10
il numero

MILANO
F. TREVES
EDITORI

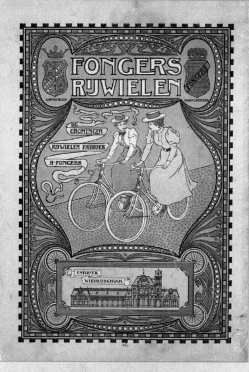

FONGERS
RIJWIELEN

DE
GRONINGER

RIJWIELEN FABRIEK
H. FONGERS

FABRIEK
EN
WINKELSCHOOL

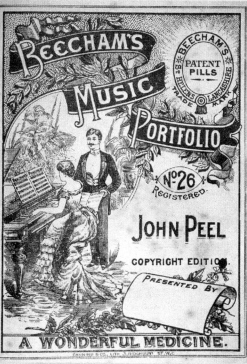

BEECHAM'S
MUSIC
PORTFOLIO

BEECHAM'S
St. HELENS
LANCASHIRE
PATENT
PILLS
TRADE MARK

No 26
REGISTERED.

JOHN PEEL

COPYRIGHT EDITION.

PRESENTED BY

A WONDERFUL MEDICINE.

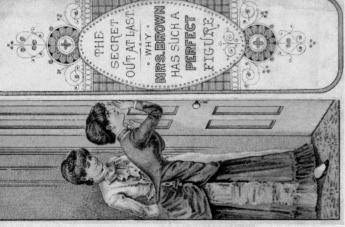

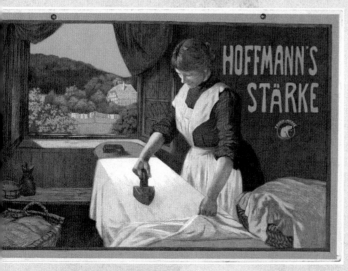

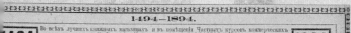

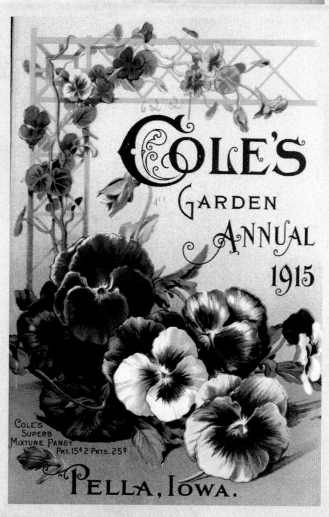

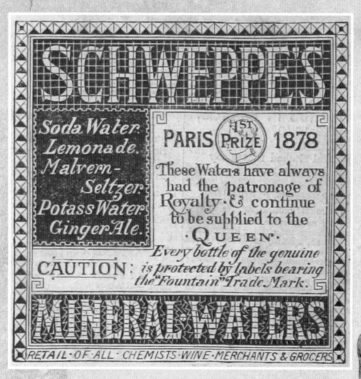

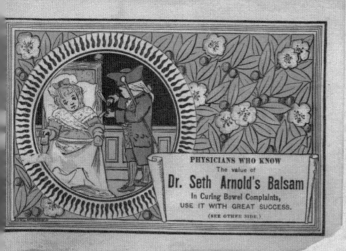

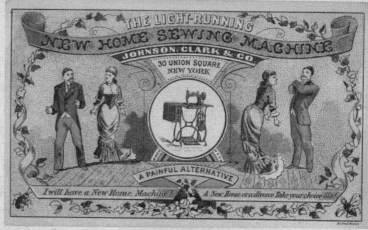

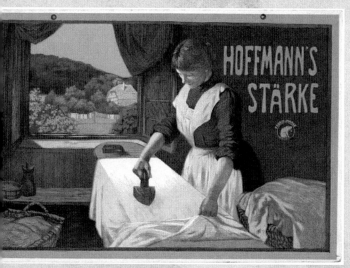

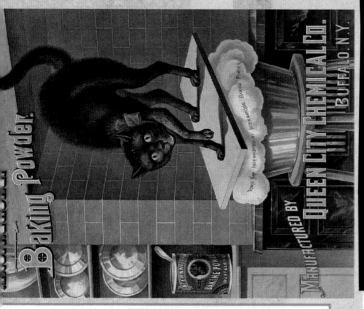

Baking Powder.

QUEEN CITY CHEMICAL CO.
BUFFALO, N.Y.

MANUFACTURED BY

JUWELIERE D'ART
MIELE & Cie

AMSTERDAM
Kalverstraat, 37

SALUTATIONS CHEZ LES PEUPLES PRIMITIFS   Fulbès tournant le dos au passant (Afrique Centrale)

Reproduction interdite

VÉRITABLE EXTRAIT DE VIANDE DE LA Cie LIEBIG

Voir l'explication au verso

The SMITH AMERICAN ORGAN AND Piano Co.

531 Tremont Street
BOSTON.

PARFUMERIE AU PRINCIPE DES FLEURS

VINAIGRE DE TOILETTE

AUX LAVANDES
DU

MONT BLANC

Préparé par

Jr. GIRAUD FILS

Parfumeur Distillateur

GRASSE, PARIS

39, Rue Etienne Marcel

MAIL
PACIFIC

THE "SUNSHINE BELT" TO THE ORIENT

If you are a poor sailor there is but one Trans-Pacific passage for you—the Pacific Mail.

Calm seas and a cloudless sky all the way, with a one day's stop at beautiful Hawaii.

Besides the climatic advantages the Pacific Mail offers all the luxury and service of the finest Atlantic steamers.

It was Secretary of War Taft's choice and should be yours.

PACIFIC MAIL S. S. CO., San Francisco, California

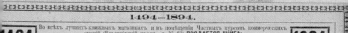

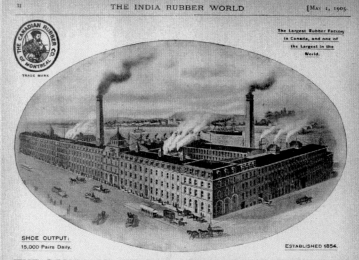

Made in the USA
Monee, IL
12 January 2021